ORGANISATION OF THE ORGANISATIONLESS:
COLLECTIVE ACTION AFTER NETWORKS

RODRIGO NUNES

A collaboration between the Post-Media Lab
& Mute Books

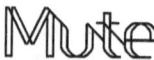

Anti copyright © 2014 Mute

Except for those images which originally appeared elsewhere and are republished here, all content is copyright Mute and the authors. However, Mute encourages the use of its content for purposes that are non-commercial, critical, or disruptive of capitalist property relations. Please make sure you credit the author and Mute as the original publishers.

This legend is devised in the absence of a licence which adequately represents this contributors' and publisher's respective positions on copyright, and to acknowledge but deny the copyrighting performed by default where copyright is waived.

Please email mute@metamute.org with any details of republication

Co-published as a collaboration between Mute and the Post-Media Lab, Leuphana University.
PML Books is a book series accompanying the work of the Post-Media Lab. http://postmedialab.org

Print ISBN: 978-1-906496-75-3
Also available as eBook 978-1-906496-82-1

Distribution Please contact mute@metamute.org for trade and distribution enquiries

Acknowledgements

Series Editors Clemens Apprich, Josephine Berry Slater, Anthony Iles and Oliver Lerone Schultz
Layout Raquel Perez de Eulate
Design Template Based on a template by Atwork

PML Books

The books in this short series are:

Claire Fontaine, *Human Strike Has Already Begun & Other Writings*, (ISBN 978-1-906496-88-3)

Felix Stalder, *Digital Solidarity*, (ISBN 978-1-906496-92-0)

Clemens Apprich, et. al., *Provocative Alloys: A Post-Media Anthology*, (ISBN 978-1-906496-94-4)

Clemens Apprich, et. al., *Plants, Androids and Operators: A Post-Media Handbook*, (ISBN 978-1-906496-96-8)

V.M., *Irational.org's Traum: A Psychoarchaeological Dramaturgy*, (ISBN 978-1-906496-98-2)

The PML Book series is just one of several outlets for the Lab's exploration of post-media strategies and conditions, which includes fellowships, a virtual lab structure, multiple collaborations, events, group readings and other documentation.

For more information see: www.postmedialab.org/publications

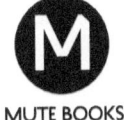
MUTE BOOKS

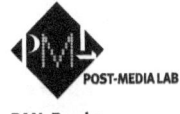
PML Books

The Post-Media Lab is part of the Lüneburg Innovation Incubator, a major EU project within Leuphana University of Lüneburg, financed by the European Regional Development Fund and co-funded by the German federal state of Lower Saxony.

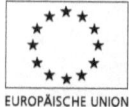
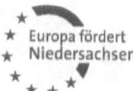
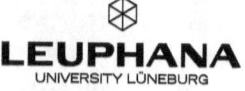

CONTENTS

Introduction: The Organisation of
the Organisationless 7

Network-System and Network-Movement 15

Distributed Networks and Distributed Leadership 31

Conclusion: Acting with the Flow 41

Introduction: The Organisation of the Organisationless

A global political moment began on 17 December 2010 in the small Tunisian town of Sidi Bouzid, when a young street vendor by the name of Mohammed Bouzizi set himself on fire in protest against the repeated humiliations he had suffered at the hands of local authorities. The moment has since spread to Egypt, much of the Mahgreb and Mashreq, to Spain, Portugal and Greece, to the United Kingdom, Israel, Québec and Chile, the United States and Mexico, and more recently to Turkey and Brazil.[1] Even if its lasting impact is yet to be decided, one could legitimately expect to see it added to a select list that includes 1848, the decolonisation struggles of the 1950s and 1960s, 1968, and the alterglobalisation cycle of the turn of the century.

For obvious reasons, it is to the latter that the present cycle can be more closely compared. There are important differences, of course. Where the moment opened by the Zapatista uprising of 1 January 1994 cracked the triumphalist façade of neoliberal globalisation, the one we are going through now came in the wake of the greatest capitalist crisis in almost a century. Where the first addressed a transnational sphere and structures of global governance, the second is more clearly circumscribed to the national sphere, opposing austerity measures, dictatorial regimes and the lack of responsiveness and permeability of political systems in hock to cronyism and world finance. Where one focused mainly on how affluence in the global North was sustained by immiseration in the global South, the other faces a growing divide between rich and poor across the board, and alarming levels of impoverishment even in the global North.

The similarities are nonetheless unequivocal: the distrust of representative politics and representation in general, the shunning of formal organisations and the tendency towards organising in networks, the preference for creative, extra-parliamentary forms of action, the tactical diversity, and the use of the internet for organising, mobilising, disseminating information, generating affect and garnering support.

In this last regard one is tempted to compare the two by saying that a historical fact has come around twice: the first time as potential, the second as actuality. For even if the alterglobalisation cycle made much of the web as one of its key differentials in relation to what came before (in the organisational suppleness and capacity to transcend physical barriers it afforded), the expansion of internet access, the advent of the web 2.0 and the coming of age of a generation that grew up online represent a qualitative leap in terms of the political appropriation of digital media.[2]

The 'choice' for networked, internet-reliant organising can only be partially understood as a 'free choice' in the fuller sense. It is true that a rejection of formal organisational ties – seen as almost inevitably leading to the formation of hierarchies, bureaucratisation, lack of transparency and the democratic deficit denounced in contemporary representative systems – is an important part of the 'spontaneous philosophy' of movements in this century. But what enables and strengthens the resolve to avoid these formal structures is the fact that, because of the internet, co-ordinated collective action is seen as possible without them. More than this, it is what people *already* do on a daily basis, it is what they already do with friends and families independently from and before doing politics. A network logic structures the everyday lives of most people, from the way they work to how they interact in their leisure time, so that networked organisation is literally what 'comes naturally' to them – which makes it easy to understand why they would see formal organisation as an avoidable, unnecessary risk.[3]

To speak of the *organisation of the organisationless* is to attempt to describe in its general outlines what exactly it is that 'comes naturally' to people when they organise in this way; but to do so as independently as possible from the 'spontaneous philosophy' with which they explain what they do to themselves. It is not that the latter is unimportant or false; the point is rather that, being a political ideology through which actors justify and legitimate what they do, it slips furtively across the border between descriptive and prescriptive registers. It is important to keep descriptive and prescriptive theories apart not because the first are 'real' while the second are made-up (both are theories, and therefore constructions constantly tested against reality), but because we need to keep our ideas of 'how things are' as distinct as possible from our ideas of 'how things should be' if we are to get a clearer sense of how, if at all, we can make the former into the latter. The effect that such a project should produce is neither bafflement nor surprise, but recognition: if anything discussed here is at all hidden, it is hidden in plain sight, and quite often it is the interference of prescription on description that will have kept it from view. First and foremost among the things that will have been so obscured is precisely the fact that what is characteristic about today's movements is not the *absence* of organisation, but a mode of organisation that can be described in its own right.

It is not that activists are somehow blind to what they do. Their 'spontaneous philosophy' is itself the product of an agonistic context in which a counterintuitive collusion between partisans *and* detractors of networked organisation, aided by the superficial accounts propagated by mass media, works to create a mystified picture of the actual practices that people are engaged in. The more one pole defines itself in opposition to the other, the less it is possible to maintain the middle ground in which questions that could be pertinent to both – how to balance openness and the aptitude for concerted action, how to be capable of strategic decisions while retaining democracy – could appear. As a result, detractors ignore the potentials for, and concrete examples of, concerted action and strategic decisions that networked organisation displays, and progressively reduce it to a caricature of inefficient woolly liberal do-goodingness or ham-fisted anarchistic obtuseness. Partisans, in turn, by making networks into a plain reversal of the shortcomings associated with traditional, formal structures (hierarchies, bureaucracy, rigidity, lack of participation and accountability), progressively tend to discuss them not as they actually are, but in accordance with the ideals that they are expected to personify or enable (absolute horizontality, leaderlessness, openness, transparency, democracy, etc.). As a consequence, whatever contradicts or qualifies such ideals will be treated as contingent, accidental and temporary. At worst, this results in a bad faith that clings to the ideals while systematically discounting or disavowing the realities of practice;[4] a refusal to pose, even if in different ways, some of the problems raised by opponents, and a difficulty in coming to grips with some intrinsic properties of networks that simply cannot be wished away. A mirror reaction takes place on the side of the detractors, who often reduce all possible organisational alternatives to a single one (the party). The upshot is that not only do the two camps become entrenched, so does the falsification that sustains their strict division.

This is a problem for at least two reasons. The first is that, regardless of whether one is *for* or *against* them, whatever solution to organisational and strategic problems can be expected today will in all likelihood come *from within networks*. This is not just because distrust of formal organisations is justifiably at an all time high, given the acute crisis of representation laid bare by the financial debacle, and the feeble response offered by most of the institutional left. It is also, and more crucially, because networked organisation is an everyday reality for everyone, *including those who oppose it on principle*, and is widely perceived as rendering formalised ties, if not obsolete, then at least not unavoidable. To put it somewhat more dramatically: *even if* a return to the party-form were found to be the solution, the party would no doubt have to emerge from existing networks. Yet given that strategic thinking has to take into account (at the very least) the 'algebraic', 'biological' and 'psychological' factors involved in the accomplishment of a goal,[5] and given that the psychological or human factor is simply not there at present (most people neither want nor think they need it), the party makes for an unlikely strategic goal, at least in the short or medium term.[6] Either way, networks should therefore have precedence.

The second reason has already been stated: the non-debate between the *for* and *against* camps, and the distorted picture of what we do that results from it, has become a hindrance to posing questions concerning the exercise of power, political organisation, and how to effect social change, and to finding the ways in which these can be posed in a new situation. We are certainly not lacking in urgent reasons to do so.

A description of the 'spontaneous' forms of organisation that those who avoid formal organisations fall into – one that is as free as possible from normative interference, value judgements, wishful thinking and moralising overtones – is a necessary step in opening the space in which to pose these questions. It may be that, for the sake of clearing the way, the time has come to be openly polemical and say once and for all that networks are not and cannot be flat; that prefiguration cannot be a goal in itself; and that an idea like horizontality may have moved from a fresh, critical antidote to outdated ways of organising, to becoming an *epistemological obstacle*.[7] 'There comes a time when the mind prefers what confirms its knowledge over what contradicts it, that is, the answers over the questions',[8] and an 'intellectual and affective catharsis'[9] may be needed to set it in motion again.

Get rid of horizontality and replace it with what – the central committee? Democratic centralism? Evidently not. The point is not to abandon horizontality, prefiguration and other ideas, which are worthy ones even if their use might be only regulative, but to get rid of precisely the binary scheme by which to criticise or relativise one thing is necessarily to slip into its opposite. It is a matter of opening the space *between* the two that makes it possible for something, being both to some extent, to be neither. Or rather, to show that the space is already there and has always been, that these mixed states are in fact the only ones that actually exist, and that we stop ourselves from fully understanding what it is that we are doing when we try to shoehorn it into such either/or oppositions. To say that leadership exists in networks while absolute horizontality does not has nothing to do with the fantasy of 'hidden leaders' that functions, in the discourse of the media and the political class, as the underside of the fantasy of throngs of previously unrelated individuals magically coming together around a goal. But since the main 'sticking point' between the two camps are issues around leadership, representation, closure etc., if it is possible to show that such phenomena are equally impossible to avoid in networks as they are in formal organisations, even if they occur in each case in different ways, some progress will have been made in establishing a set of questions and a mode of questioning pertinent to both camps. The discussion ceases to be about how to achieve absolute horizontality, which will have been demonstrated to be impossible, or how to eliminate leadership, representation and closure, and becomes about how to *negotiate* them, what *balances* to strike between openness and closure, dispersion and unity, strategic action and process and so forth. To decide that, because absolute horizontality is impossible, unaccountability and authoritarianism are justified, would be acting like the man who, 'on realising that the mind is not eternal or immortal, ... preferred to be mad and to live without reason.'[10]

It is necessary, finally, to escape the oscillation between the one and the many that much contemporary political thought appears to be stuck in.[11] Grammatically, it consists in always opposing a singular to a plural term (like identity and singularities), although it can be found at work behind the ways in which other conceptual binaries are mobilised, from the more obvious (unity and multiplicity, totality and proliferation, people and multitude) to the less so (party and movement, verticality and horizontality, transcendence and immanence). To *open* the space in which questioning can take place is also to *point* to a space between the binding of plurality into a one and unbound multiplicities: the intermediary scale of clusters, hubs, collective identities, vanguard-functions etc. – a whole bestiary that is overlooked if we jump only from one extreme to the other.

Ultimately, the point of arrival for the kind of enquiry proposed here is the question of how strategic thinking and acting is possible in networks.[12] The way it is phrased already suggests that not only are there answers, but these are to be found in immanent potentials already given in networks, and which can be further developed as the self-comprehension of networked movements develops; it is *because* networks cannot be absolutely horizontal that the question admits of an answer. For the moment, however, the goal is more modest: to propose a mode of analysis and a few conceptual tools which, by serving to further this self-comprehension, can also facilitate ways of thinking that explore those potentials. The latter task, for reasons that do not need to be explained, is necessarily a collective one.

Network-System and Network-Movement

At the height of the alterglobalisation moment, activist collective The Free Association posed the anything but straightforward question: 'what is the movement?' Appropriately, the answer was anything but straightforward: 'We do not think we can conceive of "the movement" as a thing, as an entity [a noun] which can be defined. Instead, we are thinking of the movement in terms of the *moving* [verb] of social relations.'[13]

There are obvious difficulties in employing the concept of 'movement' to describe moments such as the present one.[14] The word inevitably suggests some degree of cohesion or community regarding goals, identity, practices and self-awareness – all of which would seem to be lacking, or present only in the vaguest sense, in the cases at hand. On the contrary, these cases seem to subsume several different movements – their goals, identities and practices – acting in greater or lesser synergy, with more or less coherence, in a single conjuncture. This is a first problem, cognitive as well as political, faced by attempts to apply the concept of movement to these phenomena: the risk of either doing violence to their overall diversity, by making one part stand in for the whole, or being capable of grasping them only in terms too generic to be of much use.

That Hardt and Negri's concept of 'multitude' gained as much traction as it did around the turn of this century was no doubt related to its seeming capacity to solve this problem. At once one and many, deployed in the singular but denoting a plurality, *the* multitude is 'a multiplicity, a plane of singularities, an open set of relations, which is not homogeneous or identical with itself and bears an indistinct, inclusive relation to the outside of it.'[15] The concept's subsequent fall from grace, however, might just as well be explained by its inability to really escape the oscillation between the two. Anyone who, when asked about the agency behind any political event of the last decade, replied only 'the multitude', though perhaps not wrong, would be ultimately not saying much. Invoked in this way, the concept clearly has far more evocative than explanatory power. Ultimately, Hardt and Negri's abhorrence of 'mediation' (reductively identified with sovereignty, unity, totalisation, identity, transcendence) seems to deprive them of the means to speak of the *intermediary* level at which 'the multitude is formed through articulations on the plane of immanence without hegemony' – that is, precisely, through mediations.[16] One notices a symptomatic change in how the words 'immediate' and 'immediately' occur from *Empire* and *Multitude* to *Commonwealth*, a book in which the question of the multitude's 'becoming-prince' – its aptitude for political subjectivation and strategic action – looms large. Whereas in the first two books they usually appear in a positive association with the multitude's constitution,[17] in the latter we find it in various contexts of negation.[18] This indirectly signals a second problem of employing a singular 'movement' as a descriptor here: by blurring the internal differentiation of what it describes, it blurs the interactions among its components, which is where coordination and decision making take place.

A third problem is highlighted by the Free Association:

> By thinking about movement(s) [as thing-like entities], we end up privileging those groups which have been identified

in advance as 'political formulations' and fail to see the ways in which the majority of the world's population – 'activists' and 'non-activists' – exists both within and against capital.[19]

Sensitivity to these questions could be taken as indicative of both the legacy of 1968, with its preoccupations with diversity and expansion of the concept of the political, and of a novelty that appears with the alterglobalisation moment: the effort to bring network thinking to bear on social movement (self-)reflection, already announced in Subcomandante Marcos' address to the First Intercontinental Meeting for Humanity Against Capitalism that took place in Chiapas in 1996. If, as Marcos claimed, '[w]e are the network, all of us who resist', and if most people resist on a daily basis and everyone is connected to everyone else in some way, where do we draw the line? [20]

Network-System

There are several difficulties when it comes to individuating a network in order to analyse it. First of all, there is the issue that networks are dynamic, acquiring and losing nodes and ties, developing and reconfiguring clusters all the time. Any description of it can aspire to being no more than a freeze frame of a continuous process. The problem is made worsens if we add qualitative considerations as to the changing *nature* and *strength* of ties in it.[21] Then there are limits regarding our capacity to compile the relevant data; while this is less of an issue when dealing with platforms like Twitter, it is a huge obstacle if the object is social networks in the strict sense, i.e., those whose units are individuals or groups of individuals. Because of this, but also because there would be diminishing returns to indefinitely extending the field of analysis, it is necessary to define criteria of what counts as a relevant sample, artificially reducing the fuzziness of the boundaries we are dealing with. And of course, first and foremost, we must define what counts as a node and what counts as a tie for the purposes of analysis.

That the individuation of a network is definition-dependent does not make networks 'subjective'. The relations that constitute them objectively exist, at least as far as the compiled data-set will tell us, but it is only once some definitional criteria have been provided that those relations are revealed. For example, we can describe a hashtag network on Twitter, where the nodes are Twitter accounts, regardless of whether they are individual or collective identities, and the ties are tweets or retweets containing the hashtag. It will thus include everyone 'talking about' that subject during the relevant timeframe, regardless of what they were saying, unless we fine-grain our criteria further. Whatever it can tell us about node centrality (which nodes were the most retweeted, which retweeted the most) is restricted to that network alone, and only when this analysis is examined against other hashtag networks can a more reliable picture emerge of the most influential and best connected on Twitter according to a broader criterion. Since we all belong to several networks at once, and since each part of a network is also a network, we can individuate an indefinite number of networks at an indefinite number of scales. Whatever results we find will be relative both to the definition and the scale (an important hub in a local network may be a minor hub in a broader network; a relatively sparse network can appear as a relatively dense cluster within a sparse network…).

If the criteria we choose determine what boundaries we see a social network as having, thus presiding over inclusion and exclusion, the political stakes of our choices become evident. This is a challenge brought into sharp focus by the upheavals of recent years, in which the sudden eclosions of mass mobilisation involved far more people than those who would define themselves as 'activists', and by our highly mediatised contemporary environment, in which information and affect can spread and produce effects well beyond the physical barriers of proximity, personal acquaintance etc.

To take one example, in September 2013, footballers in Brazil started a self-described 'movement' called Bom Senso FC [Common Sense FC], which demanded changes to the national football calendar and player / club relations. It is likely none of those involved took part in any of the protests seen since June, towards which only a few footballers have publicly expressed sympathy; yet the connection between the players' initiative and the contestatory atmosphere in the country escaped no one. Moreover, the forms of industrial action adopted by the movement have since been copied by basketball players. The question, then, is: should football and basketball players be counted as part of the Brazilian 'movement', even when it is doubtful many of them would do so themselves? If not, why? Because they do not recognise themselves as such? Because they did not participate in any of the movement's more easily recognisable expressions – a fuzzy boundary in itself? And if yes, can we really stretch 'movement' that far?

Clearly, a new grammar is needed. Perhaps one can be produced by differentiating between *network-system*, *network-movement* and *movement(s)*.[22]

A network-system is a system of different networks – of individuals, of groupings (temporary or permanent, formal or informal), of social media accounts (individual and collective), of physical spaces, of webpages (corporate outlets, blogs) – which constitute so many interacting layers that can neither be reduced to nor superposed on each other. Each of these layers contains its own sets of ties of different natures and strengths, nodes, clusters and so on, even if their topography is generally isomorphic; each is dynamic, so that the validity of any descriptions is time-bound. Individual persons, while themselves constituting a network that can be isolated as a layer (or several, according to criteria), are also the elements that circulate among layers. It is because individuals form groups, interact on social media, frequent physical spaces and webpages etc. that the different layers connect. It suffices that an individual exists in *any one* of these layers to belong to the network-system; this makes the objection that not everyone has access to the internet or social media moot for the purposes of this definition. There is no dichotomy between digital media and the 'real world'; they constitute different, but interacting layers.[23] Finally, just as parts of networks are also networks, network-systems are embedded and overlap with one another: the Diren Gezi network-system is embedded in a Turkish network-system, which overlaps with other countries' wherever there are ties to Turkish nationals, expats in Turkey, and so on. The global Anonymous network-system can be somewhat artificially broken down by country or region, and a United States Anonymous network-system embedded in it will heavily overlap with the Occupy Wall Street network-system, and so forth.[24] 'Network-system' thus allows us to look beyond explicitly or self-identified political expressions, as well as any suggestions of shared goals, practices etc., and to picture a broader 'moving' of social relations. It is, so to speak, a movement as it exists *in-itself*, its capacity to produce effects existing independently from its being consciously registered by all who belong to it.

What, however, would entitle us to say that Brazilian footballers belong to the network-system created by the June protests, as opposed to merely the national network-system of Brazil? Reference, precisely, to an *event* – in this case, the still nameless event that began in Brazil in June 2013. Events create their own network-systems out of pre-existing ones, by creating (or destroying) nodes and ties, changing the nature and strength of ties, determining the formation, transformation or disappearance of clusters, reconfiguring the interactions within and between layers. It is a 'moving of social relations' in a very literal sense. This is why it is legitimate to speak of 'virality' in relation to them, by analogy with the way in which viruses exploit existing networks for their replication (using long-distance travellers as hubs that allow it to reach distant corners, for example) while also creating new ties (people need not be acquainted in order to contaminate each other). An event is a process of contagion whereby a sensible change, first actualised in a relatively small number of bodies, words, actions (for example, the occupiers at Gezi Park in Istanbul), becomes, by virtue of those actualisations, communicable to ever larger numbers of people who come across it either by direct contact in the physical layer (people, places) or mediated contact through other layers (corporate media, social media). In this case, what spreads and replicates is at once information – words, images, narratives, actions etc. – and the *affective charges* that travel with it.

Affective Synchronisation and Performativity

One of the distinctive traits of the present moment is precisely the way in which our heavily mediatised environment drastically enhances the reach, velocity and insistence (capacity to continue producing effects) of information and affect. This is more than a quantitative difference; it is a change in degree that produces a change in nature. It makes a huge affective difference that developments can be followed in real time, both because little of the affective charge is lost, and because response time is reduced: a sense of urgency can be produced even over large distances, and acting on it is an immediate possibility. As informative and affective resonance increases across layers, the sense of urgency grows in intensity, and an *affective synchronisation* occurs that envelops ever more people.[25] The combination of affective synchronisation, strength in numbers, and seeing those with whom they have strong ties join the protests lowers the *thresholds of participation* for ever more individuals, generating a cascade effect that is perfectly performative: because something is happening, I join in and get others to join, ensuring that there will be *more* of whatever is happening. As the event is replicated in a myriad other, smaller scale events (small local actions, or even just people telling friends about their experience at a protest, or hearing about it in the news), the network-system is created.[26]

The amplitude of an event of this kind will be proportional to how successfully it taps into a social malaise that has brewed for some time without finding any outlets, such as the social impacts of economic stagnation, as in Europe and the US, or the social costs of economic growth, as in Turkey and Brazil. The more public the expression of this malaise becomes, the more people are likely to see the need and the possibility of moving from indignation to action. The more people manifest a disposition to act, the more widespread it becomes. This is the *performative* dimension of digital media, functioning like a battery that accumulates energy to be discharged in the streets, used to great effect in cases like Egypt's 'We Are All Khaled Said' Facebook page. While 'clicktivism' has been (rightly) criticised from different quarters, when this kind of process approaches a critical threshold, there is a growth in the number of ties and a progressive strengthening of ties that amounts to an overcoming of 'clicktivism'. This could be described in Facebook terms as a passage from 'like' to 'share' and 'friend', then 'comment' to 'confirm participation', and finally actual participation in actions, online and offline, at which point new, non-digitally-mediated, strong and weak ties will be created. At the same time, the expanding digital layers of the network-system function as a space in which ideas can be circulated and 'tested' (through metrics such as 'likes' and retweets) as potential candidates to the role of 'structural germs' which provide focal points and basic protocols for collective action.[27]

This much social media can do. However, it takes a dose of magical thinking to believe that an initiative can function as such a 'germ' without it being prepared in sufficient detail and given at least a minimal structure in order to make it viable. A process that could superficially seem like a miraculous convergence of previously unrelated individuals requires, in fact, various more tightly knit networks that play a structuring role online (by managing popular pages and accounts, for example) and offline (by setting locations, dates, times, themes, visuals, protocols – 'peaceful', 'militant', 'no flags', colour-coded – working out basic infrastructure and so forth).[28] There is not a single, sweeping wave of quantitative increase and intensification of ties, but a more complex movement in which stronger tie clusters and the organisational consistency they afford are essential to structuring both the technologically mediated contagion and what goes on 'on the ground'.[29]

The collective identities of these more tightly knit networks may exist prior to and independently from the event itself, or be created at its earliest stages. In the latter cases, as in Spain and the United States, they will tend to define the event to a greater extent, and function as the 'root identities' (Occupy Wall Street) from which later collective identities will derive (Occupy Oakland, Occupy London, Occupy Sandy, Occupy Data).[30] In the former, such as Egypt and Brazil, they will be subsumed as clusters in the larger network-system; Mexico's #YoSoy132 would appear to be somewhere between the two. This entails political and topological differences in the resulting network-systems – those of the Egyptian and Brazilian kind tending to be more neatly divided into clusters, with pre-existing clusters playing a more prominent role; those of the Spanish and North American kind tending to be more organised around new collective identities, resulting on greater emphasis on the event's novelty (of agenda, practices etc.).

Network-Movement

It could be objected that there is a circularity in saying that it is the event itself that justifies including in that event's network-system developments whose participants would not necessarily recognise themselves as a part of it. There are two answers to this. To the extent that there is a truth of the event that is only subjective – it is only those for whom an event has happened that can see its different effects and ramifications – we can say, with Spinoza, that this truth is *index sui*, an index or evidence of itself. On the other hand, while it is true that, insofar as network individuation is definition-dependent, the individuation of a network-system is itself a political construct, and such a construct is at once the index of a subjective truth *and* open to argumentative judgment as to whether the relations it illuminates are objectively real.[31]

Any description such as 'Egyptian Revolution network-system' or 'Diren Gezi network-system' is a *reflection on* the given network-system. That is, while they are obviously produced from within that network-system, and thus presuppose its existence, they exist at a second-order, reflexive level in which the network-system consciously apprehends itself. If the network-system is the 'movement' in-itself, this level is the 'movement' for-itself. We can call it the *network-movement*: the conscious, self-reflexive understanding held by some that the multiple elements and layers assembled in the network-system constitute an interacting system of actors, intentions, goals, actions, affects etc., however heterogeneous these may be. The network-movement is at once the act of self-recognition that takes place when people start talking about 'the movement' to refer to these heterogeneous elements, and the ensemble that they have in mind when they do so. Everyone who belongs to the network-movement belongs to the network-system, since belonging to the former means, first of all, being aware of oneself as belonging to the latter. But not everyone who belongs to the network-system participates in the network-movement. It is this element of 'expanded' self-awareness – at once awareness of oneself and of the larger system of which one is aware of being part – that provides the criterion to distinguish between the two.

We can now see more clearly the advantage of replacing 'movement' with 'network-system' as a point of departure. To begin by trying to identify 'the movement' makes it difficult for us to go beyond the network-movement; counting beyond those who count themselves in seems dubious. This creates a bias in favour of those more consciously political expressions, and efforts to expand it further tie us in the sorts of knots we saw above.[32] As a result, we are at once left without a language with which to speak of various other phenomena, and with an inadequate tool with which to evaluate the conjuncture as a whole.

Starting from the network-system, we can then differentiate a network-movement within it – ultimately, a subnetwork of individuals who have a more or less clear and distinct self-awareness of belonging to a 'movement' that is a network whose parts are themselves networks. We can then discern different movements that exist within that network-movement: subnetworks that can be singled out according to a social base ('the labour movement'), a political orientation ('the anarchist movement'), an identity ('the indigenous movement'), an issue ('the movement against welfare cuts'). They evidently overlap with one another, and the same individual may belong to several in different capacities, through ties of different natures and strength. Finally, within these movements we can isolate several subnetworks which may be groups of friends, more or less permanent collectives, more or less formalised groups, adepts of this or that kind of tactic, trade unions, parties etc.[33] The mode of analysis proposed here thus allows us to see *organisation* as a continuum stretching from lesser to greater degrees of *stabilisation, formalisation* and *consistency*. Stabilisation denotes here the development, by habit, of tacitly endorsed rules, authorities, structures, from a couple of more influential Facebook pages or Twitter accounts to a defined membership, process etc. Formalisation is understood as meaning the development of explicitly stated and agreed rules and structures regarding leadership, decision-making etc. Finally, consistency refers to such things as the capacity to produce and enforce decisions, to grow in an ordered way, durability, discipline etc. This means both that there is no such thing as 'no organisation' and that parties, unions etc. are describable as networks independently of their own forms of stabilisation, formalisation and consistency, even though these will undoubtedly determine their form and functioning as networks, and the more so the stronger they are.

If, however, we define the network-movement as a self-reflexive relation that parts of the network-system have to itself, does that mean it exists only in some people's heads? Yes and no. In one sense, it possesses a multi-perspectival existence, in that different actors, according to the limits of their knowledge (i.e., the actors and ties they are aware of) and of the definitions they employ, will determine its boundaries differently, if dynamically. There may be as many network-movements as there are people who recognise its existence. On the other hand, most of the ties and interactions that their idea of the network-movement will include are such that their actual existence can be described without reference to the network-movement; for example, an action by one set of actors creating an opportunity for another group. Besides, due to the transitivity of relations, A might not be aware of C, but in interacting with B, which interacts with C, may belong to the network-movement as seen from the perspective of B and C, even if it only includes B in its own; the network-movement does not depend on reciprocity. In this regard, the network-movement *really is* everyone who sees themselves as part of a system whose internal interactions of whatever kind define a boundary between itself and an external environment with which it interacts as a system – even if not *every single node* sees *every other single node* as belonging to it.

Ultimately, the network-movement lies somewhere between a statement of fact and a political project, or several. It has to do with a decision as to how far and to whom we extend our recognition, as well as our feelings of solidarity and comradeship. That some protesters denounce and distance themselves from those they see as 'violent' or illegitimate means that, while they recognise the latter as part of the same network-system, they refuse to extend solidarity and comradeship to them. Of course, to see others as part of one's own movement does not entail agreement with everything they do, but involves a fundamentally different approach to disagreement – in this case, for example, the object of disagreement would be tactics rather than the borders separating lawful and unlawful behaviour. Ultimately, how broad one's conception of the network-movement is determines how comprehensive a picture one has of the overall field of struggle, the direct and indirect interactions within it, the impacts that actions might have, latent connections to be developed, ties to be strengthened, differences to be taken into account, struggles and objectives to be prioritised, points of leverage, areas in which intervention is called for.

As such, the network-movement is a prerequisite for strategic and tactical thinking. Whereas 'the movement' inevitably implies some presupposition of a unity that is not given, 'network-movement' starts from a dynamic multiplicity – a dynamic system whose parts are also dynamic systems – and points towards the continuous project of the construction of *commons*, temporary or permanent, whose form is not presupposed in advance. The choice for either dispersion or unification is *not* inscribed in advance in the notion of a network-movement. On the contrary, the idea of network-movement opens the possibility that several ways of combining the two – swarming, distributed action, diversity of tactics, institutionalisation, forking, even (why not?) parties – can be selected according to what the occasion requires. Once these are considered in the context of a network-system, the point is not what solution is *valid for* the whole, but what solutions *work within* the whole. There is no need to find a single answer to what everyone must do – it is no wonder these should appear unlikely, given the number of variables being dealt with, but instead the need to find the mediations which, through their interaction, enhance the whole system's capacity to act. The point is to create something more than mere alliance building (where the parts, understood as constituted groupings of people, are supposed to stay the same, only co-operating punctually) and less than a one-size-fits-all solution (e.g., the idea of the party). This is about strategic interventions that can attract both constituted groups and the 'long tail' that does not belong to any groups, pitched not as exclusive but as complementary, whose effects can reinforce each other.

Distributed Networks and Distributed Leadership

As can be gleaned from examining graphs of interactions in the more easily measured digital layers, and as most participants will know from experience, the network-systems that emerged from the struggles of the last years display some ubiquitous characteristics of networks: 'short chains [or paths], high clustering, and scale-free link distributions.'[34] The latter specifically means that *node degree* (the number of ties each node has) is subject to a *power law*, a statistical distribution generating a curve in which a relatively small number of highly connected nodes (hubs) is followed by a sharp drop to a long tail of nodes with slowly decreasing node degrees. Among the first to observe the same phenomenon across various different kinds of networks were Albert-Lázló Barabási and Réka Albert, who proposed in 1999 a model of network formation that directly connects growth and scaling: as (most) networks expand, they produce this kind of statistical disparity.[35]

So this would be the bad news: our networks are not only unequal, they are so by mathematical necessity, and this is directly connected to how they develop. The consequence is inescapable: if by 'horizontality' we mean a situation where each node would have exactly the same degree or weight in a network as every other node at any given time, networks *cannot* give us that. That they cannot is not contingent or accidental, nor a temporary condition to be overcome, but an *intrinsic property* of what they are and how they grow. This does not come without good news, however. Firstly, the presence of power laws is widely recognised by scientists as a likely sign of a self-organising system. (Though, it must be stressed, networks do not appear to self-organise their way *out of* power laws.) Secondly, this kind of network – called *scale-free* because it has no 'average' nodes to speak of – occupies 'a sweet spot between the unbuildable and the unusable', in that it is because of highly connected hubs that clusters can communicate with each other through counterintuitively short paths between distant nodes, the so-called 'small-world' effect.[36] This also makes scale-free networks 'highly resistant to random damage, since the average person doesn't perform a critical function' and so only a selective attack to several hubs at once could take them down.[37]

This places the network-systems of current struggles somewhere between the last two models put forward by Paul Baran, the 'decentralised' (each cluster presided over by a hub) and the 'distributed' (mesh-like).[38] Yet while topological models are important, as they indicate generalisable properties, a graph is only a static image; we need to take the dynamic aspect into account. Apart from the continuous appearance and disappearance of nodes, these network-systems also display the continuous formation, transformation and dissolution of clusters, the continuous quantitative and qualitative transformation of ties, and consequently the continuous appearance, growth, shrinking and disappearance of hubs, from the quantitative point of view (number of ties) as well as the qualitative (their nature and strength). Besides, the proliferation of ties constantly produces *redundancy*, creating alternative paths between nodes that counteract the tendency for hubs to become critical to the network's functioning.[39] This *continuous internal differentiation* entitles us to describe them as distributed, even if, especially in their sparser peripheries and among small-degree nodes, we have something closer to a decentralised architecture.

To sum up: these are not *horizontal movements*, but *distributed network-systems* – whose participants may or may not espouse the ideal of horizontality – which are subject to continuous internal differentiation. Regardless of what individuals' ideas about decision making, leadership and representation might be, and the practices that they derive from these, their general and most constant framework of interaction is best described, from the point of view of the system, as *distributed leadership*. It is not that there are no 'leaders'; there are several, of different kinds, at different scales and on different layers, at any given time; and in principle anyone can occupy this position.[40] That is, they are not leader*less* but, if the poor wordplay can be forgiven, leader*ful*.

While this has always been true, to a certain extent, of any movement at any point in time, what is unique about the present is the way in which the 'mass self-communication' afforded by digital media has radically enhanced it.[41] The potential for real-time diffusion and amplification that exists today has enabled a *diffuse vanguardism* in which initiatives can snowball exponentially and produce impacts far exceeding their original conditions.

But what does 'occupying a leadership position' mean? There are two senses in which this can be interpreted, according to whether we treat leadership as *property* or as *event*.

Distributed Leadership: Hubs and Vanguard-Functions

The simplest quantitative way to evaluate leadership as a network property is node degree: the more ties, the more capacity to influence other nodes. In *directed* networks – those in which ties are unidirectional, as in the internet, where a link in a webpage points to another webpage – a distinction can be drawn between *out-* and *in-*degree. This, in turn, determines a distinction between *hubs* and *authorities*, hubs being nodes with a high out-degree (they point to several other nodes), authorities being nodes with a high in-degree (several other nodes point to them). 'Authorities' are so called because, while hubs are more central to interaction in the network-system, distributing more traffic and connecting more clusters, it is towards authorities that a lot of traffic and therefore attention is directed, theoretically making them more 'influential' (for example, the most cited papers in academic citation networks).

These quantitative measures, however, indicate a *potential*, not necessarily its exercise.[42] In fact, an important conclusion that follows from the dynamic nature of networks is that the *continued existence of potential* is to some extent dependent on its *successful exercise*. If a hub ceases to interact and route relevant traffic, its ties might go dormant or disappear, and traffic may be routed around it, reducing or eliminating its importance in connecting different clusters. If it routes bad traffic (spreads false information, misleads its 'followers', supports negative initiatives), it might have, if not necessarily a quantitative decrease in degree, a qualitative loss in trust or reputation.

A clearer picture of power relations in a network-system can only emerge once we introduce considerations as to the *quality* of ties – their nature and intensity. For example, it will often be the case that corporate media outlets will function as authorities, just by virtue of being the first to provide webpages that can be linked to, or because they are readily recognised sources, etc. In activist networks, however, the material will normally be shared with (and sometimes because of) comments directly criticising or contradicting the content. Equally, two people in a network may have the same number of ties, but one of them will have developed deeper relationships, thus enjoying more trust and a greater ability to influence others. Characteristics that are less strictly relational (capacity to inspire and motivate, charisma, empathy) evidently also come into play.

Leadership occurs as an event in those situations in which some initiatives manage to momentarily focus and structure collective action around a goal, a place or a kind of action. They may take several forms, at different scales and in different layers, from more to less 'spontaneous'. This could be a crowd at a protest suddenly following a handful of people in a change of direction, a small group's decision to camp attracting thousands of others, a newly created website attracting a lot of traffic and corporate media attention, and so forth. The most important characteristic of distributed leadership is precisely that these can, in principle, *come from anywhere*: not just *anyone* (a boost, no doubt, to activists' egalitarian sensibilities) but literally *anywhere*. That is, such events do not necessarily have to go through any large scale decision making process, which is perhaps not so good for a certain conception of egalitarianism. Of the three most iconic square occupations of 2011 – Tahrir, Puerta del Sol and Zucotti – only the last one was ever decided at an assembly, and even then an assembly much smaller than the occupation itself would then constitute. This simple observation puts paid to the portrayal of these movements as driven by large assemblies. More often than not, large assemblies *result from* initiatives, not the other way round.

General assemblies were and are important for the running of occupied spaces, for the amount of connections afforded by concentrating a large number of people in one place at one time, for generating and maintaining affective intensity.[43] Ascribing too much centrality to them is, however, to remain somewhat stuck in the one/multiple oscillation (through the assumption that, once constituted, they should by right become the 'sovereign' deliberative space in their 'jurisdiction'). Upholding them as a prefigurative model, besides, is to overlook the serious obstacles to scalability and generalisability that they present.[44] Assemblies may or may not happen against the background of distributed leadership, which, being a property of the network-system, *must* happen; excessive focus on them amounts to reducing the network-system to the movement-system, and the movement-system to only one of its expressions.

A successful initiative is not one that manages to capture the support of the entire network-system, but one that attains *sufficient* support to produce at least the effects it intends; success is relative to scale. If we consider the creation of the overall network-system ('Egyptian Revolution', '15M', 'Occupy Wall Street') as a root event, these initiatives are events *internal* to these network-systems, which in turn generate their own network-systems, embedded in the root one. Thus, for example, the network-system that had begun to be created in the run up to the Spanish protests of 15 May 2011 was made denser, expanded and given new content by the camps (*acampadas*) that sprung up all over Spain following Madrid's Puerta del Sol. Puerta del Sol thus became a local network-system, and sparked a country-wide *acampadas* network-system, all of which are subnetwork-systems that expanded, made denser and added new content to the 15M network-system. Each *acampada* is in turn an event in its own right, creating its own local network-system, and so forth. This idea of successive nesting explains why, after many obituaries of Occupy Wall Street had been written, Occupy Sandy managed to organise a highly sophisticated disaster response operation in very little time. While OWS had disappeared as a 'movement', the network-system it had created remained strong and active enough for an initiative to be able to activate it and develop a new subnetwork-system out of it very quickly.

While Albert and Barabási's generative model, originally developed from a study of the World Wide Web, was successful in explaining the occurrence of power/law distributions by directly associating them to network growth by means of the notion of *preferential attachment*, it soon showed a serious flaw. Preferential attachment – the law according to which a more connected node will tend to attract disproportionately more links from new nodes added to the network, thus increasing their degree while degrees along the long tail remain low – can account for hubs. It cannot, however, account for those cases in which a 'poor node' moves from the periphery to the centre, or a relative latecomer rapidly increases in degree.[45] It cannot elucidate something like the rise of Google. This demanded the development of a new model capable of accommodating individual qualitative differences, which was done by assigning each node greater or lesser *fitness* in its environment.[46] However, since what will often define a node's advantage over others is that it introduces a true, unpredictable novelty, and not a response to a previously noticeable lack, 'fitness' is worth far more as an *ex post* explanation than a predictive tool. We can apply it to phenomena in the network-systems we are dealing with, however, provided we bear in mind that it pertains to a node's initiative more than to the node itself, whose centrality may or may not increase as a result of the initiative's success.

This possibility – that a node which is not a hub may act as a vector of collective action in ways that largely exceed its previously measurable potential to influence others – is the flipside of how hubs can decrease as well as increase in status. In order to differentiate these events from the 'ordinary' activity of highly connected hubs (distributing traffic, directing attention etc.) we can say that, in these cases, a node or cluster temporarily occupies a *vanguard-function* in relation to the network-system. The vanguard-*function* differs from the teleological understanding of vanguard whose sway over the Marxist tradition helped engender vanguardism. It is objective to the extent that, once the change it introduces has propagated, it can be identified as the cause behind a growing number of effects. Yet it is not objective in the sense of a transitive determination, which would be made necessary by historical laws, between an objectively defined position (class, class fraction) and a subjective political breakthrough (consciousness, event). The vanguard-function is akin to what Deleuze and Guattari call the 'cutting edge of deterritorialisation'[47] in an assemblage or situation; opening a new direction that, after it has communicated to others, can become something to follow, divert, resist etc.[48]

Distributed leadership is therefore to be understood as the combination of a topological property (the presence of hubs) and two dynamic ones (hubs can increase and decrease, and new hubs can appear or, alternatively, nodes can 'lead' without necessarily becoming a hub or authority in the process). If the first of these entails that networks are constitutively unable to become the perfectly flat, totally transparent, absolutely horizontal media they are sometimes posited as at least potentially being, the latter two indicate the measure of democracy they can be said to have. Individual networks can of course be more or less democratic according to how distributed leadership potential is, and how open they are to new initiatives and hubs emerging. It is only if we understood 'democracy' as synonymous with 'absolute horizontality' that they could be called undemocratic. Horizontality, despite being an impossible goal to achieve, has its use as a regulative principle, indicating the need to cultivate the two dynamic properties of distributed leadership.

Because their capacity to influence fluctuates, hubs are subject to a process of *continuous legitimation* that depends on their own activity (whether they remain active and continuously distribute traffic deemed relevant), on the development of the network itself (since the appearance of other hubs can decrease their centrality), and their perceived *network ethic* (whether they are seen as acting co-operatively and in the interest of the whole network-system, or only with a view to securing and enhancing their own power).[49] In times as highly suspicious of representation as ours, the tendency is for hubs with a greater leadership potential to be more severely scrutinised, since people are both wary of what may happen if a node becomes too big, and instinctively aware that a hub's power can be controlled by suspending co-operation – in social media terms, 'unfriend', 'unfollow', 'unlike'.[50] This in no way makes distributed leadership an ideal market of information and initiative: fitness does not exclude preferential attachment, and preferential attachment inevitably slants the 'market' in favour of hubs; whoever is more connected is more likely to be heard. But it shows in what way distributed leadership can be said to offer a concrete instantiation of the Zapatista motto of *mandar obedeciendo*: 'to rule by obeying.'

Conclusion: Acting with the Flow

The guiding question proposed at the start was: how is strategic thinking and acting possible in networks? While answering it was not an immediate goal, I hope that the mode of analysis proposed here, and the new objects and levels it has tried to make visible, can place it on more promising ground. It is because network-systems do not oscillate between a (possible or impossible) one and a (purely unbound) multiplicity, but are continuously differentiating themselves internally into clusters, hubs, collective identities, vanguard-functions etc., and because these elements interact with each other in a context of distributed leadership, that the space exists for thinking outside of the false dichotomy between either unification from above *or* a catallaxy of spontaneous interactions producing the best possible results. There is a place for strategic interventions which are not aimed at totalising the network-system, but do not leave things in the hands of a blind 'process' that is presumed virtuous. We have seen that there is no telling in advance what can occupy a vanguard-function at a given time. Is it possible, however, to plan oneself into that position, and not just for a momentary swarming against a target, but in a more durable way?[51]

The question naturally turns from 'how?' to 'who?' *Who does the strategising?* The answer is, ideally everyone. Not that every individual or group should be their own leader, of course. There is nothing strategic about having a vision of a desired transformation and the steps needed to produce it, or a certain set of principles as to what constitutes political action, and to apply them indifferently, regardless of the situation and whoever

Conclusion: Acting with the Flow

else one is interacting with. In any collective sport, a good team is neither one in which one player organises the whole game, nor one in which each player does their own thing, but one in which all players are equally aware of all the movements on the pitch, and capable of occupying whatever spaces need occupying – even when that means staying put.

Coming as it did in the context of a resurgence of the left after the debacle of really existing socialism, the appeal to networks as a descriptive and normative category often functioned as a way of eliminating the 'who?' question through proliferation. The flatness of networks ensured the impossibility of the *transcendence of agent over process* characteristic of vanguardism: no-one was the leader because no-one *could* be the leader; totalisation was impossible. However, if we erase the strategic, intentional dimension of agency, rather than situating it within a system, we end up instating a *transcendence of process over agent*, ascribing agency to the process itself. But the network-system is no more than what agents do, the interactions between what they do, and the interactions between itself and its 'outside'. The *de facto impossibility of totalisation* does not abolish the need for *partial syntheses* that try to apprehend it in order to discern possible courses of action. For what it's worth, the sporting metaphor indicates two qualities that strategic thinking in a network-system must encompass: *complementarity* and a *care for the whole*. It is through an awareness of a diverse ecology of agents and interactions and the political potentials offered by the conjuncture that interventions can be devised. These require neither exclusivity nor adherence to a programme or group identity, but can nonetheless mobilise, structure and coordinate the collective behaviour of parts of the network-system according to a certain strategic wager with relatively well-defined ends in sight.[52] This is what those initiatives have done that managed to break the deadlocks in which some of the network-systems in question found themselves after the period of occupations, such as the Plataforma de Afectados por la Hipoteca and 15MpaRato in Spain, or the Rolling Jubilee in the United States; or those that induced the creation of network-systems, such as Movimento Passe Livre and other groups organising the struggle around public transport in Brazil. These have successfully combined a denser, more consistent organising core with relatively open structures and moments that could involve a 'long tail' of less active nodes in various different capacities (from crowdsourcing to swarming, from mass demonstrations to distributed actions), in some cases attaining a social legitimacy well beyond the ranks of 'activists'.

'Care for the whole' – taking into consideration the network-system's development and capacity to act as a whole, and not of this or that node or cluster within it – does not entail treating diversity as an absolute value or seeking lowest common denominators as a way to avoid divisions. But it creates divisions not by stating a programme but by creating a practice, and avoids turning the assertion of divisions into the assertion of identities. Not everyone needs to back an initiative, although it requires support proportional to its aims; but what is backed is not a group or position that exists outside the strategic wager which the initiative embodies, but the wager itself. This amounts to occupying the vanguard-function, or being a vanguard, without vanguardism.

Conclusion: Acting with the Flow

Much more can be said about the properties that make up the 'fitness' of a strategic initiative: a 'plausible promise' that it can develop into something relevant for the system as a whole and its goals;[53] a balance between openness and closure (closed enough that its basic purpose and protocols are clear, while open enough that newcomers feel they can make it their own); offering different possibilities of involvement according to different thresholds of participation and capacities (tactical diversification and functional differentiation); acting across layers; correctly identifying points of leverage and possessing some degree of directionality (a sense of progression from immediately achievable to more ambitious goals). These are all *formal* properties, abstracted from any particular content, the articulation of which was admittedly the main goal here. More still can and must be thought about what, in each conjuncture, would be feasible strategic wagers worth pursuing, as part of a deliberate collective effort to develop the immanent capacities of the network-systems that exist today, and to exploit the possibility that, between acting as though one were outside of what one acts upon, and 'going with the flow', a third alternative may be given: acting with the flow.

Footnotes

1 Since every beginning happens at least twice, one could equally pinpoint the date as 10 November 2010, when a breakaway group from an 'official' march stormed Conservative party headquarters in London, generating a rapid radicalisation of the UK student movement. An even earlier precursor would be the 10 January 2009 protests that kickstarted Iceland's 'Silent Revolution'.

2 An odd feature of the debate on the causal role of digital media in recent protests is that it often seems to revolve around the (patently absurd) claim that they were created and determined in their content by these media. On the other hand, the causal role of digital media is beyond question in providing 'the very infrastructure that created deep communication ties and organizational capacities in groups of activists before the major protests took place, and while street protests were being formalized.' Modified. Phillip Howard and Muzammil Hussain, 'Democracy's Fourth Wave? Information Technology and the Fuzzy Causes of the Arab Spring', 27 March 2012, 14, http://ssrn.com/abstract=2029711

3 Clay Shirky analyses this in economic terms as a collapse of the costs of group formation that entails a loss in the relative advantages of institutionalisation – since activities that would previously require institutions can now be pursued with much lither co-ordinating structures. Clay Shirky, *Here Comes Everybody: The Power of Organizing Without Organizations*, London: Allen Lane, 2008.

4 I use 'bad faith' here in the strictly non-moralistic, Sartrean sense of self-deception. On this, see Gerbaudo's observation that 'social media have become a means through which leadership is exercised while at the same time concealed, so as to maintain an impression of absolute spontaneity and fulfil the criteria of horizontalism.' He cites the case of 'the "HQ" of Occupy Wall Street, an office space near Zucotti Park, where a dozen activists worked on communication': 'people were not trying to make the presence of a group of core organisers a completely hidden secret. What was scandalous [...] was not the presence of organisers, but the fact that

[they] were housed in a specific space, instead of being invisible in the crowd or hidden [...] somewhere in town.' Paolo Gerbaudo, *Tweets and the Streets: Social Media and Contemporary Activism*, London: Pluto 2012, p.144.

5   See Thomas Edward Lawrence, 'The Science of Guerrilla Warfare', in *Encyclopaedia Britannica*, 10: 950-953, Chicago: Encyclopaedia Britannica, 1951.

6   It could be objected that the goal of (at the very least) 'activating the emergency brake' on global capitalism is equally unlikely; the problem, however, is that what putting all eggs in the party basket seems to do is place one unlikelihood as a precondition for another.

7   See Jo Freeman's assertion that '[t]he idea of 'structurelessness' [...] has moved from a healthy counter to [the hierarchical structuring of society and "the continual elitism of the Left"] to becoming a goddess in its own right.' Jo Freeman, 'The Tyranny of Structurelessness,' available at: http://uic.edu/orgs/cwluherstory/jofreeman/joreen/tyranny.htm.

8   Gaston Bachelard, *La Formation de l'Esprit Scientifique*, Paris: Vrin, 1957, p.15.

9   Ibid., p.18.

10 Baruch Spinoza, *The Ethics*, Samuel Shirley (trans.), Indianapolis: Hackett, 1992, Sch., Pr.41, V.

11 To be precise, the issue is not multiplicity as such, but the automatism whereby the opposite of unity can only be thought as *unbound* multiplicity that cannot be arranged or grouped in any ways. We can think this in terms of the party-movement opposition: not only is no party ever really *the* one (it is one among many), no movement is ever really *just* multiple (it is not only made of differences between individuals/singularities, but also of differences between clusters of individuals/singularities). Even Alain Badiou's thought, which originally set itself as a (dis)solution of the one/many problem, seems to return to it by positing an option between *the* Idea of communism and sheer dispersion: 'Lacking the Idea, the popular masses' confusion is inescapable'. Alain Badiou, *The Communist Hypothesis*, David Macey and Steve Corcoran (trans.), London: Verso, p.258.

12 Before we begin, it should be made clear that 'networks' refer here to more than social media, encompassing

networks of individuals, infrastructure, keywords etc. While social media offers us the most readily available network visualisations, owing to the relative ease with which the relevant data-sets can be obtained, it constitutes, as we shall see, only one layer among several. It is equally taken for granted that no single layer can map perfectly onto any other: the network of people on Twitter is different from the network of people on the streets, even if the variance between one and the other may itself vary according to internet access, platform diffusion and technopolitical appropriation. It is the case, however, that all the layers have the same kind of topology; they are *not* identical, but are *isomorphic*.

13 The Free Association 'What Is the Movement?', *Moments of Excess: Movements, Protest and Everyday Life*, Oakland: PM Press, p.28.

14 On why to speak of 'moment' rather than 'movement', see Rodrigo Nunes, 'The Global Moment', *Radical Philosophy* 159, 2010, pp.2-7.

15 Michael Hardt and Antonio Negri, *Empire*, Cambridge, MA: Harvard University Press, p.103.

16 Michael Hardt and Antonio Negri, *Commonwealth*, Cambridge, MA: Harvard University Press, 2009, p.169. This issue can be thought in relation to another criticism often levelled at Hardt and Negri's work: even if 'not homogenous or identical with itself', treating the multitude as singular risks obscuring the very real and politically significant phenomena of class stratification inside it.

17 For example: 'When human power appears immediately as an autonomous cooperating collective force, capitalist prehistory comes to an end.' Hardt and Negri, *Empire*, p.366.

18 For example, the 'affirmation of immanence is not based on any faith in the immediate or spontaneous capacity of society'; 'the organization of singularities required for political action and decision making is not immediate or spontaneous'; 'economic capacities are not immediately expressed as political capacities.' Hardt and Negri, *Commonwealth*, p.15, p.175, p.365. This, it should be noted, does not come with a reevaluation of mediation; despite the new emphasis on the *instituent* dimension of constituent power, 'mediation' is still understood as external to the

multitude – the sheer fact of which is indicative of how, in this context, 'multitude' operates as singular, not multiple, i.e., internally differentiated/mediated.

19 The Free Association, 'What Is the Movement?', p.30.
20 Subcomandante Marcos, 'Tomorrow Begins Today: Invitation to an Insurrection', in *We Are Everywhere: The Irresistible Rise of Global Anticapitalism*, Notes from Nowhere (ed.), p.37, London: Verso, 2003.
21 I have chosen to speak of *ties* and *nodes* (which stresses that these are not necessarily individuals) throughout. By 'nature' I mean the different kinds of ties that individuals can have (friend, acquaintance, relative, colleague, subordinate), and by 'strength', their differences in intensity. Although I refer to 'weak' and 'strong' ties in the abstract, intensity is not easily or thoroughly quantifiable, and so often has more of a relative sense (one tie is *weaker* than another, but becomes *stronger* than it was before...).
22 The concept of 'network-system' has, like a piece of software code, been under cooperative development since it was first introduced by Raul Sanchéz Cedillo. See Raul Sanchéz Cedillo, 'El 15-M como Insurrección del Cuerpo-Máquina', *Universidad Nómada* 2012, http://www.universidadnomada.net/spip.php?article377; Rodrigo Nunes, 'The Lessons of 2011: Three Theses on Organisation', *Mute*, June 7 2012, http://www.metamute.org/editorial/articles/lessons-2011-three-theses-organisation; Javier Toret (org.), *Tecnopolítica: la Potencia de las Multitudes Conectadas. El 15M, un Nuevo Paradigma de la Política Distribuída*, IN3 Working Paper Series, 2013, 20, http://www.uoc.edu/ojs/index.php/in3-working-paper-series/article/view/1878. I cannot recommend enough the conceptual and empirical work done by Javier Toret and the 15M Data Analysis group on Spain's 15M, which has been a constant source of inspiration.
23 Even if an individual has no direct internet access and knows no-one who does, they are very likely to interact with it – by reading news items influenced by Twitter discussions, seeing posters produced out of Facebook memes, hearing of digitally-mediated protests... '[N]ot everyone in the world is on the internet, but everyone on the internet is in fact in the world', and so the internet can often be the shortest path to people who are not on it. See @Ciudadano_Zer0, 'El

Camino al Mundo Real', *Vaeo*, 15 August 2013, http://vaeo.es/2013/05/18/el-camino-al-mundo-real/. Of course, the amount of layers one is active in is a factor in determining one's capacity to influence the conduct of others.
24 National references are used for the sake of simplicity, as the systems themselves are evidently not constrained by national boundaries.
25 15M Data Analysis have devised ways to empirically verify affective and conceptual synchronisation through the analysis of Twitter graphs. See Toret (org.), *Tecnopolítica*, op. cit., pp.69–85.
26 According to MacAdam and Paulsen's explanatory model of participation in high risk activism, developed from an empirical study of the 1964 Mississippi Freedom Summer Project, engagement depends on 'the occurrence of a specific recruiting attempt', a tentative linkage between movement participation and one of the identities sustained by the networks of which an individual is part, 'support for that linkage from persons who normally serve to sustain the identity in question', and 'the absence of strong opposition from others on whom other salient identities depend.' We should complicate this model according to at least three factors: the facility with which ties can be created and intensified on digital networks; how the insistence of information and affect across layers can take the place of recruiting attempts; and how the proliferation and intensification of ties, combined with transindividual affective synchronisation, can override existing identities and produce new ones. Douglas MacAdam and Ronelle Paulsen, 'Specifying the Relationship Between Social Ties and Activism', *American Journal of Sociology* 99, 1993, p.659.
27 Simondon draws an explicit comparison between a far-from-equilibrium state of supersaturation, in which 'an event is ready to take place, or a structure ready to emerge', and a 'pre-revolutionary' one: 'all it takes is for a structural germ [*germe structural*] to appear.' Gilbert Simondon, *L'individuation à la lumière des notions de forme et information*, Grenoble: Jerôme Millon, 2005, p.549.
28 'Network' here stands as a general name to describe more or less formal collectives, affinity groups, assemblies like the ones that preceded Occupy Wall Street etc.

29 Gerbaudo speaks of 'liquid organising' and 'choreographic leadership' to refer to this partially closed, partially open aspect; Feigenbaum, Frenzel and McCurdy talk about 'partial organisation.' See Gerbaudo, *Tweets and the Streets*; Anna Feigenbaum, Fabian Frenzel and Patrick McCurdy, *Protest Camps*, London: Zed, 2013.
30 Javier Toret (org.), *Tecnopolítica*, op. cit., p.51.
31 For what it's worth, one of Bom Senso FC's figureheads denies direct influence, but acknowledges the 'propitious moment' created by the protests and that they might have inspired some players. See Rodrigo Martins, 'Precisamos Envolver os Jovens Atletas', *Carta Capital*, 2 November 2011, http://www.cartacapital.com.br/sociedade/201cprecisamos-envolver-os-jovens-atletas201d-4671.html.
32 A similar problem occurs when trying to speak of 'composites' like Anonymous or the Black Bloc. On one level, they are just open identities that can be freely reclaimed by anyone, regardless of prior involvement or direct contact. At the same time, these identities are not entirely open, not just in that they presuppose some adherence to a set of values, but also in that disputes can arise between interpretations of those values, resulting in exclusions or marginalisation (as in Brazil between 'left' and 'right' Anonymous collectives). On another level, 'Black Bloc' or 'Anonymous' applies to more or less loose networks that participate in operations or actions; on yet another, to more tightly-knit collectives that tend to initiate and frame those. Finally, in Anonymous' case, not only do those individuals who command large botnets possess a disproportionately large share of the collective capacity to act, there are thousands of computers that participate in Anonymous operations without their owners even being aware. Here again the concept of network-system can be useful where others that it encompasses ('movement', 'group', 'collective', 'tactic') break down. See Parmy Olson, *We Are Anonymous: Inside the Hacker World of LulzSec, Anonymous, and the Global Cyber Insurgency*, New York: Back Bay, 2013.
33 These are only the most obvious ways in which subnetworks can be isolated. But, again, there is no limit in principle to how many networks we can individuate within the same network-system (for instance, people from different groups

working on the same campaign, or people in parties, unions and collectives who know each other socially etc.)

34 Steven Strogatz, *Sync: The Emerging Science of Spontaneous Order*, London: Penguin, 2003, p.256.

35 See Albert-Lázló Barabási and Réka Albert, 'Emergence of Scaling in Random Networks', *Science* 286, 1999: pp.509–512. This became known as the Albert-Barabási model.

36 Shirky, op. cit., p.216.

37 Ibid.

38 The first one was, of course, 'centralised' (hub-and-spokes). See Paul Baran, 'On Distributed Communication Networks', 1962, www.rand.org/content/dam/rand/pubs/papers/2005/P2626.pdf.

39 As Baran observed (and visualisations show), in order to produce a decentralised network out of a centralised one, and a distributed network out of decentralised one, one has to add ties between nodes that are not hubs; that is, to increase redundancy.

40 It must be stressed that, throughout, 'leader' does not necessarily refer to individuals; on the contrary, for reasons explained above, in the physical layer at least these will often have to be groups (although, of course, one can find cores of more influential individuals inside them).

41 Manuel Castells, 'A Network Theory of Power', *International Journal of Communication* 5, 2011, pp.773–787.

42 Degree is not the only measure of the importance (centrality) of a node; it is possible to measure, for example, how connected it is to other important nodes (*eigenvector* centrality), the extent to which it lies on paths between other vertices (betweeness centrality) or its distance from other nodes (closeness centrality). For the sake of simplicity, I have disregarded these possibilities here.

43 Manuel Castells observes that 'what appears to be an ineffective form of deliberation and decision-making is in fact the foundation needed to generate trust, without which no common action could be undertaken against the backdrop of a political culture characterized by competition and cynicism.' Manuel Castells, *Networks of Outrage and Hope*, Cambridge: Polity, 2012, p.225.

44 On assemblies, see Keir Milburn, 'Beyond Assemblyism: The Processual Calling of 21st Century Left', in *Communism in the*

21st Century, Volume 3: *The Future of Communism*, Shannon Brincat (ed.), Santa Barbara: Praeger, 2013.

45 I take the term 'poor node' from Pimentel and Silveira's analysis of Facebook graphs in the early days of the Brazilian protests. Their observation is that 'momentary relevance does not necessarily lead to a rise in social network capital.' See Tiago Pimentel e Sérgio Amadeu da Silveira, 'Cartografia de Espaços Híbridos: As Manifestações de Junho de 2013', *Interagentes,* 11 July 2013, http://interagentes.net/2013/07/11/cartografia-de-espacos-hibridos-as-manifestacoes-de-junho-de-2013/

46 For the fitness model, see Ginestra Bianconi and Albert-László Barabási, 'Competition and Multiscaling in Evolving Networks', *Europhysics Letters* 54, 2001, pp.436-442.

47 Gilles Deleuze and Félix Guattari, *Mille Plateaux*, Paris: Minuit, 2004, p.298.

48 The concept applies at different scales: Mohammed Bouzizi's suicide functioning as a vanguard-function to the friends and family who start the protests in Sidi Bouzid, which in turn lead others to protest and so on; Tunisia as a vanguard-function in relation to Egypt, the Arab Spring in relation to 15M… 'As Gabriel Tarde said, one would need to know which peasants, in what regions of the south of France, stopped greeting the local landowners.' Deleuze and Guattari, ibid., p.264.

49 This is undoubtedly the main suspicion harboured against parties or party-like organisations, although it is a problem neither exclusive to nor necessarily always given with them.

50 This can serve as a factor in explaining why the formation of mass parties appears unlikely in most places today: people sense the advantage of temporary attachments over formalised ties when it comes to keeping accumulation of power in check. This does not, of course, say anything about whether temporary attachments are in and of themselves sufficient for all political purposes.

51 To do so amounts to occupying the position of 'catalyst' as described in Simona Levi, 'Notas para una r-evolución 2 (versión 1.1): Segunda fase: vicios vs nuevas virtudes tácticas', 8 July 2012, http://bancodeideas.15m.cc/profile/anonymous/texts/4ff983ed171b6b2bbf000267.

52 I develop these points in Rodrigo Nunes, 'Notes Towards

Rethinking the Militant' in *Communism in the 21st Century*, op. cit.
53 See Eric Steven Raymond, 'The Cathedral and the Bazaar', 2000, available at: http://www.catb.org/~esr/writings/cathedral-bazaar/cathedral-bazaar/.

www.ingramcontent.com/pod-product-compliance
Lightning Source LLC
Chambersburg PA
CBHW031551210526
45464CB00003B/1252